THIS BOOK
BELONGS TO

_____

_____

Published in Great Britain by World Distributors (Manchester) Limited.
A Pentos Company.
P.O. Box 111, 12 Lever Street, Manchester M60 1TS.
Printed in Italy. SBN 7235 4912 5

A LITTLE OWL BOOK

THINGS THAT GO

written by Paul Hunter
illustrated by Alan Linsdell

WORLD & WHITMAN

ON THE ROAD

Cars go on the roads.
Lots of people have cars –
big ones, little ones,
and all different
shapes and sizes.
Their engines need petrol
to make them go.

If you haven't a car of your own, and you don't want to walk, you can go by bus or taxi. Buses are cheaper than taxis, but not as quick. They have to keep stopping to pick people up.

Some people have motorbikes, mopeds and scooters.
These have smaller engines than cars, and nothing to
shelter you from the rain.

A bicycle has no engine at all. It is quite hard work pushing the pedals to make the wheels go round, especially going up a hill! Some bicycles have bells to ring, and some have baskets for the shopping.

ON THE RAILWAY

Trains go along railway lines.
People travel in passenger trains,
but there are also goods trains.

The passenger coaches or goods trucks
used to be pulled by steam engines.
These needed coal to make them go.

Now trains are pulled by diesel or electric engines instead. Diesel locomotives need diesel to make them go, but electric locomotives get their power from overhead electrified wires.

ON THE WATER

Boats and ships go on the water. Some have engines, some have sails, and some have to be rowed, using oars. The big ship is an ocean liner, and carries lots of people across the sea to other countries.

IN THE WATER

Submarines go down in the water. They are underwater vessels. People in submarines use periscopes to see above the water. Even if you can see the periscope, you still cannot see the submarine. It is hidden under the water.

IN THE AIR

Aeroplanes carry people through the sky. Some planes are big and some are small. This jumbo is very big and carries a lot of passengers all round the world. Planes land on long runways at the airports.

This is Concorde, one of the newest aeroplanes. It looks a bit like a white bird with a funny nose. It mostly goes on Transatlantic flights between Britain and North America, and it travels very fast indeed.

FASTER AND SLOWER

These all go very fast too.
The racing-car goes on special roads called race-tracks.
The speedboat goes on the water.
The High Speed Train goes on the railways.

Other cars, boats and trains go slower.
Can you think of any?

UP AND DOWN IN THE AIR

Helicopters can go forwards, up and down.
They cannot go as fast as aeroplanes,
but they can land in places where there is not much room.
They have propellers which go
round and round very quickly.
These keep the helicopters up in the air.

GOING WITH THE WIND

Some things use the wind to make them go.
Gliders and balloons go through the air.
Sand yachts have sails like other yachts,
but go along the beach instead of on the water.

OVER THE WATER

A hydrofoil skims across the sea, just above the water. It is lifted above the water on its foils, which are a bit like the wings of aeroplanes. It has an engine and propellor like other boats, but goes faster because of the foils.

A hovercraft also skims over the water. It makes itself a cushion of air to travel on, and this cushion keeps it out of the water, and helps it ride over the waves. Hovercrafts have propellers or jet engines to make them go, and big ones carry cars as well as people.

CARRYING THINGS

Ferries carry people and things across water.
They go across rivers, lakes and seas.
The large ones carry cars and lorries and coaches,
and are called car ferries.

Vans and lorries carry things along the roads.
Lorries are bigger, and can carry more.
They have a separate cab for the driver.
When this cab can be removed
from the back of the lorry,
it is called an articulated lorry.

ON THE BUILDING SITE

Bulldozers have special blades at the front for pushing earth around. Some of them have caterpillar tracks around their wheels to help them move. The one in this picture does, doesn't it?

Cement mixers don't actually go anywhere at all. They just have a drum that goes round and round to mix the cement. Sometimes cement mixers are on the back of lorries, so that they can be moved around.

You can see cranes,
diggers and tipper trucks
on building sites too.
Do you know what they look like?

ON THE FARM

A combine harvester cuts corn.
It has revolving blades at the front,
and a conveyor belt to carry
the corn to a chute at the back.
From here the corn goes into
a trailer pulled by a tractor.

AT THE FAIR

Traction engines use coal to make them go, like the old steam engines. They used to be used to pull very heavy loads. Now you can see them at traction engine rallies or fairs, looking all polished and bright.

IN SPACE

When a rocket goes up into space,
there is a countdown: 5,4,3,2,1, Blast-off!
Rockets are used to send other spacecraft into space.
Sometimes they send people called astronauts into space too.

When the astronauts landed on the moon,
they took with them
a vehicle called a Lunar Rover.
This helped them get around
more easily on the moon.